AF230049

5 Keys To Fail Proof Living

Achieve
The Life You Want

by

Stephen Lee

AuthorHouse™
1663 Liberty Drive, Suite 200
Bloomington, IN 47403
www.authorhouse.com
Phone: 1-800-839-8640

This book is a work of non-fiction. Unless otherwise noted, the author and the publisher make no explicit guarantees as to the accuracy of the information contained in this book and in some cases, names of people and places have been altered to protect their privacy.

First published by AuthorHouse 10/13/2008

ISBN: 978-1-4184-2268-4 (sc)

Library of Congress Control Number: 2004093546

Printed in the United States of America
Bloomington, Indiana

This book is printed on acid-free paper.

ACKNOWLEDGMENTS

My thoughts and theories in this book stem from my time spent reading the bible, other people experiences and everyday life lessons. I have been able to move forward positively in life by simply living and learning from my triumphs, but more importantly my defeats. I have learned from an eclectic group of people over the last 38 years which include Pastors, Teachers, Christians, Sinners, Athletes, and Criminals etc. I practice the philosophy of humbling myself to learn from any and everyone regardless of who they are or where they come from.

I would like to thank God for his love, mercy and grace.

I would also like to thank my daughters Kendal and Kennedy Lee for their unconditional love.

INTRODUCTION

Change Is Hard But Worth It In The End

This book is based on my life lessons as I have traveled throughout life. I'm not a pastor, psychologist or expert, I'm just like you an individual who got tired of being sick and tired and made some drastic changes in my life to improve myself and my future. I share this with you because I am an ordinary guy and I know that if I can make changes and improve my life I'm here to let you know that you can do the same. I tailored this instructional manual to appeal to average everyday people like me and you. This is an informational manual that can be read in a couple of hours, but you can also keep this with you to help with your day to day journey. This manual will help you make the changes you need to achieve the life you really want.

As you read and digest this spiritual information take time out and meditate on the information and slowly implement the suggestions into your life. I guarantee if you are willing to take control of your life you will achieve the life you deserve.

TABLE OF CONTENTS

Key 1 Let Go Of Your Past   1

Key 2 Renew Your Mind   9

Key 3 Set Goals   17

Key 5 Share Your Testimony   33

Key 1

Let Go Of Your Past

The first thing I realized I had to do in order to achieve the life that I wanted was to let go of my past. All the things, people and places that were not helping me move to a more prosperous and abundant life, I cut out of my life. What I want to share with you in this chapter is the first step to achieving all you want in life and more. Below are some helpful hints to help you eliminate unproductive things, people and places from your life:

A) You can't make progress in life as long as you are holding onto bad habits or clinging on to your past.

B) Your past affects your future. Anything negative you did in your past will result in negativity in your future. Any positivity you sowed in the past will result in positivity in your future.

C) Don't live in your past. Your past mistakes do not dictate your future.

D) Learn from your past mistakes to help guide you through the present.

E) Rituals, habits and practices that resulted in positivity continue to utilize.

F) Make sure you learn from the experiences of others both positive and negative.

G) Remember we all have a past and everyone deserves a second chance.

HOW TO OBTAIN
THE RELATIONSHIPS YOU WANT:

Whether you want to obtain prosperous friendships, marriage or working relationships the first thing you need to do is ask yourself what do you want out of the relationship. Once you decide what you want out of each relationship then start giving to others what you want for yourself. If you want love show love, if you want affection show affection, if you want respect show respect. Giving to others will always put you in a position to receive. Next forgive others that have hurt you in the past as well as ask for forgiveness from those that you have hurt in the past. Lastly and most importantly forgive yourself for how you behaved in past relationships. Implementing these changes will set you on your way to obtaining fruitful and prosperous relationships in any environment.

HOW TO OBTAIN
THE FINANCES YOU WANT:

First things first. Look at where you are now in regards to your financial situation. Do you have debt? Do you know your net worth? Etc. Once you know where you are financially, look at how you got there. Critique your spending and saving habits. If you are not currently financially prosperous meaning debt free with some sort of savings,(IRA's, mutual funds and/or 401k accounts) you need to stop and correct your spending habits. If you don't have a budget create one that you can stick to.

If you are not saving start saving even if it is $20.00 a week a least you are starting to put money away for your future. If you eat out every weekend tone it down to once a month. Start taking lunch to work instead of eating out for lunch. What I'm trying to say is change your old spending habits and make some sacrifices to obtain the financial results you want. Don't worry about how much money you don't have concentrate on how much money you will have.

Key 2

Renew Your Mind

The second key I feel that is important is the renewing of your mind. In order to change you must be willing to let go of negative thought processes that you grew up believing. Some of the behaviors we were taught by our family and friends are not always productive. Really evaluate what you have been taught and make sure that your thoughts and ideas are assisting you in obtaining the prosperous life you deserve. Below are some helpful hints to help you with achieving a new mind set:

A) Question the way you think about everything.

B) Change negative ideologies that you thought were right from your upbringing.

C) Be selective of what you expose yourself to (people, places and things).

D) Always choose to do good over evil.

E) Keep changing your life for the better regardless of who ridicules you.

F) Aggressively remove negative influences from your life.

G) Envision in your mind what type of person you want to be and strive for that.

H) Tell those close to you of your change so they can hold you accountable to changing.

I) Take time out once a week to reflect and make sure you are making the appropriate changes in your thinking.

J) All renewal begins and ends with God. He reveals truth to us and enables us to respond to that truth.

HOW TO OBTAIN
THE RELATIONSHIPS YOU WANT:

To obtain the relationships you want you must do things that you thought you would never do. Everything you thought was dorky, nerdy or stupid must now become everyday habits and gestures you must display. For example if you are a person that doesn't like to say hello early in the morning to your friends, love ones or co-workers. You will now need to renew your mind and give morning salutations when you don't want to and in return those same people will be friendly to you. If you are a person that is not an affectionate person to your spouse you will now need to give your spouse a hug, kiss or just hold their hand in public to improve your relationship. What I'm saying is you need to come out of your comfort zone and think differently to get different results than you received in the past. Renew your mind today. Today is a new day.

HOW TO OBTAIN
THE FINANCES YOU WANT:

In order to change your financial situation you need to evaluate the way you think about money. Change your mindset on how you spend and how you save. If possible pay cash for all purchases, when you use credit cards you are putting yourself in deeper debt unless you can pay off your credit card purchase within 30 days. Train your mind to stick to a budget as well as a savings plan. If your mindset is geared towards budgeting, savings and decreasing debt you will eventually manifest those thoughts into reality. Whatever is on your mind and in your heart is what you will become. If you see yourself as a budgeter, saver and debt free that's what you will become. Renewing your mind about money will renew your finances.

Key 3

Set Goals

The third key to achieving the life you want is to set goals for yourself to accomplish. It is hard to change anything without goals to get you to your end result. Goals help us to stay focus on our dreams. Goals also give us a sense of reward as we accomplish them. Goals keep us motivated to complete the task at hand. I have a few helpful hints to keep you focused on the goals you will set to help you achieve and obtain the life you really want:

A) Patience is the key to achieving your goals.

B) Obtaining goals may take some time.

C) Don't give up on obtaining your goals.

D) Before pursuing a goal make sure it's worth your time.

E) Your goals should benefit others in some way.

F) Don't let anything distract you from obtaining your goals.

G) Pray for guidance about your goals.

HOW TO OBTAIN

THE RELATIONSHIPS YOU WANT:

Put on paper what type of relationship you want, whether the relationship is romantic, professional or platonic. Once you write it on paper then you can strategize how you are going to obtain the relationship. Get yourself a calendar and give yourself due dates for certain tasks to complete to get you closer to the relationship you want. For example, have a due date at the end of the week to schedule lunch with a person at work that you feel you want to establish a relationship with. Another example, go to your church or any church you feel comfortable with and ask for information about their "Singles Ministry". Once you get information about the singles ministry and the events the church facilitates for singles; make sure you sign up for at least one event per month. This will put you in the environment to meet someone romantically as well as platonically. You are now strategizing a way to get yourself into the game of relationships. You can't get what you want in life if you don't put yourself in the environment to achieve it.

Strategize, attack and seize the relationships you want.

HOW TO OBTAIN
THE FINANCES YOU WANT:

The first step is to devise a plan to get out of debt if you have debt. Get a calendar and start with the lowest debt balance you have and give yourself a monthly payment plan to pay on that debt (if possible make double payments). This monthly plan will lead you to decide on a payoff date for the entire debt, which will lead you to the next bill or debt to pay off. It's like a snowball effect; if you pay off one bill then you will have the confidence to pay off other debt. Next you need to save for your future. 401K's, IRA's, 403B's are all good resources to start saving for retirement. If you know you will be retiring in the next 10, 20, or 30 years you need to figure out how much money you will need to survive when you retire. Regardless of when you will be retiring please start setting goals monthly and yearly to get your savings and or retirement accounts to the appropriate amount you will need at retirement. Setting goals to get out of debt and saving for your future will get you on your way to financial freedom.

Key 4

Give Back

The fourth key to achieving the life you want is "Giving Back". If you want to live a fulfilled life always try to give back in every aspect of your life. Give money to churches and community organizations. Also volunteer your time, resources and knowledge. Giving back to help improve the lives of others is like a drug, once you try it and experience the joyous feeling, you want to experience that feeling all the time. When ever I had problems of my own that were hard to deal with and I wanted relief from my issues, I would look to help others with their problems. By assisting others I was able to get away from my problem for a while and help someone else, after I helped the other person my problem or issue didn't seem so bad. Listen to the old saying "It is better to give than to receive". Below are a few helpful hints to assist you to give back to others:

A) Be a joyful giver.

B) Give the first 10% of your earnings to God.

C) Give to charities (donate food, clothing,etc.).

D) Volunteer time in your community.

E) Share knowledge and wisdom with those who ask.

HOW TO OBTAIN
THE RELATIONSHIPS YOU WANT:

Giving back to help others always helps to achieve the relationships we want. As you give to others and are assisting in improving their situations you are always in an environment of power. Whether you are in church or at work or volunteering in a community center, as you are giving you are around people who you want to have relationships with. Who better to have a working relationship with than someone who has the same beliefs that you have. Who better to have a romantic relationship with than some one who has the same interest that you have. What I'm saying is that the people you are around while you are giving back are most likely giving back as well. My experience has been when you have two or more givers working together the more both individuals are able to receive. Keep yourself surrounded by positive people, who want to give to others, you will find that these people are the ones you want to have relationships with.

HOW TO OBTAIN
THE FINANCES YOU WANT:

As I suggested earlier make sure you give your first 10% of your income to God, this way you are setting yourself up for the opportunity to receive more income from God to sow into the world. Next make offerings or donations to the church or community organization of your choice. When you give above and beyond your required

10%, you are setting yourself up for a harvest above and beyond anything you have ever seen. You may not get a truck load of money, but God will see that you have favor in your life, whether it be job security, a promotion or favor with someone to give you money.

Finally, share knowledge and wisdom when ever possible, by doing so God will assure that you receive specific financial knowledge that you need at a specific time in your life. Plan on giving back financially for a year like I suggested and see how you finances improve. "It never hurts to try".

Key 5

Share Your Testimony

The fifth and final key to obtaining the life you want is sharing your testimony. After you complete the first four keys and make the necessary changes in your life, make sure you share your journey with others. This is why I chose to write this book. What other way to help people and share my life lessons than to publicly put them on paper. When you share your successes with others it gives them a sense of hope that they can accomplish that same success. Let's face it. The only reason we are here is to help others reach their full potential. My plea to you is to either share this book with another person or share your testimony with them. Remember "Each one teach one". Below are some helpful hints to help you share your story in order to help others:

A) Relate your testimony to the Creator.

B) Always share what God has done for you.

C) Avoid discouragement when sharing.

D) Don't be afraid to share.

E) Share with the intent to help others.

HOW TO OBTAIN
THE RELATIONSHIPS YOU WANT:

When you share with others you break down barriers of communication. I'm not saying to tell others you want relationships with all your deep dark secrets, but by sharing certain information a person wouldn't normally know will give you a chance to build relationships with them. Discuss family, community or job related successes. Sharing also gives others the impression that you are upfront with no hidden agendas. Try sharing who you are with others. The more you share the more you may receive.

HOW TO GET
THE FINANCES YOU WANT:

Share financial knowledge and information with others who have the same financial mindset you have or who have the financial knowledge you want to obtain. Sharing financial information is a great way to educate others and yourself at the same time. Sharing information is as old as the barter system. Sharing goods and services was the quickest way to achieving results when you didn't have the money to pay for certain things. What I'm saying is you must share information with others to get information you don't have. This way everyone is obtaining information that is assisting in obtaining the finances we all desire. Remember "A mind is a terrible thing to waste".

About The Author

Stephen is an average guy who was determined to change his life. He took it upon himself to make some drastic changes to achieve the life he felt he deserved. Now as Corporate Executive Stephen prides himself on reaching out to others to assist them with achieving the life they desire. Please use this information to improve your life and help others along the way. May God Bless You.